Seasons Through the Year

Each day when I go out to play,
I look to see the kind of day.
Will I need a coat or hat?
Or is it much too hot for that?

I've been checking days for over a year,
And I have found a pattern here.
Seasons come and seasons go,
Bringing sun or rain or snow.

Spring, Summer, Autumn, then Winter days
I watch my world change in predictable ways.

Jill Norris

1

Let's Learn About
Seasons Through the Year

Using Literature Books

Your library is filled with good books that support the theme *Seasons Through the Year*. Check out as many as you can and put them in a library center in your classroom. The illustrations and the language will be important resources for student writing. Read at least one book a day to your class. Make the book available for students to reread. Encourage students to bring books about seasons from home to share with the class.

Bibliography

Here are a few good choices:

A Forest Year by Carol Lerner; William Morrow and Company, 1987.

As The Earth Turns Fall by Lynn M. Stone; Rourke Book Co., 1994.
(Also available: *As The Earth Turns Spring*, *As The Earth Turns Summer*, and
As The Earth Turns Winter)

Caps, Hats, Socks, and Mittens by Louise Borden; Scholastic Hardcover, 1989.

Exploring Nature Around the Year by David Webster; Julian Messner, 1989.
(Also available: individual volumes for Fall, Spring, Summer, and Winter)

Good Morning, River by Lisa Westberg Peters; Arcade Publishing, 1990.

Molly's Seasons by Ellen Kandoian; Cobblehill Books, 1992.

The Mare on the Hill by Thomas Locker; Dial Books, 1985.

Naomi Knows It's Springtime by Virginia L. Kroll; Caroline House, 1993.

Seasons by David Bennett; Bantam Little Rooster, 1988.

Summer is... by Charlotte Zolotow; Abelard-Schuman, 1967.

Sunshine Makes the Seasons by Franklyn M. Branley; Harper & Row, 1985.

Year After Year by Bill Binzen; Coward, McCann & Geoghegan, 1976.

What Comes in Spring by Barbara Savage Horton; Alfred A. Knopf, 1992.

When Autumn Comes by Robert Maass; Henry Holt & Co., 1993.
(Also available: *When Spring Comes*, *When Summer Comes*, and *When Winter Comes*)

Why Do We Have Different Seasons? by Isaac Asimov; Garath Stevens, 1991.

Room Environment

As you set up your classroom, choose one wall or bulletin board that you can use throughout the year in connection with your "Changing Seasons" theme. Change the board as the seasons change. Provide baskets, tubs, and trays to hold real items that are signs of the current season. You may want to include items that can be used for math manipulatives.

Autumn

It is autumn.

fall
leaves
frosty
harvest
yellow
red
orange

Winter

It is winter.

Snow
sleet
ice
white
shovel
flakes

Spring

It is spring.

windy
bloom
grow
kite
fresh

Summer

It is summer.

sun
swim
play
camp
shine
sea

What Causes the Seasons?

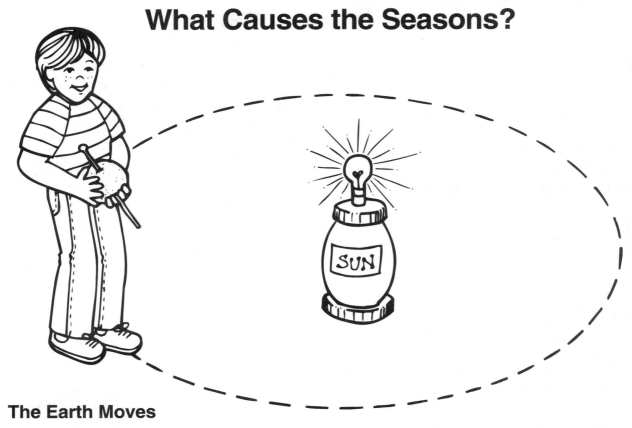

The Earth Moves

Understanding the seasons requires understanding the way that the earth moves around the sun. Help your class to visualize how this all works by using a working model. Poke a knitting needle through the center of an orange. The orange will represent the earth. The knitting needle will represent an imaginary axis or turning point. Use the light bulb in a lamp to represent the sun.

Day and Night

The earth's axis is tilted at about 23 1/2 degrees and always points toward Polaris, the North Star. Demonstrate how the earth is tilted by holding the knitting needle at a slant. Hold the orange at the same level as the light bulb. Now turn the orange around. Have students notice how the sun (*light bulb*) shines on one side of the earth (*orange*) while the orange remains dark on the other side.

The earth turns around every day.
This causes day and night.

Circling the Sun

Continue turning the earth (*orange*) on its axis and walk in a large orbit (*circle*) around the sun (*light bulb*). Explain that the earth moves in an orbit around the sun.

The earth moves in a big circle, or orbit,
around the sun. It takes a whole year
(365 days) to complete the circle.

The Sun's Rays - Direct or Slanted?

Sometimes the light from the sun shines directly on a certain spot. Sometimes the light seems to slant toward the spot. Demonstrate this idea of direct rays verses slanted rays using a flashlight and a box lid. Darken the room. Shine the light on the lid. Notice the area where the light rays hit the box lid. (*It should be a circle of bright light.*) Now hold the flashlight in the same place and tilt the box lid. (*The rays of light hit the lid at a slant. The area of light is spread out and not as bright.*)

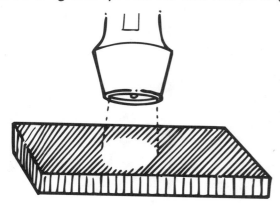 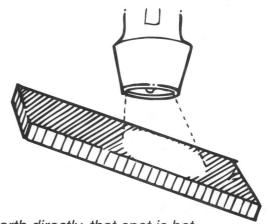

When the rays of the sun hit a spot on the earth directly, that spot is hot. When the rays hit a spot on the earth at a slant, they are spread over a bigger area. That area will not be as hot. In fact, it might be very cold.

Seasons Are Different in Different Places

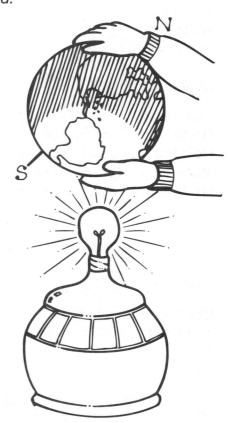

Point out the northern and southern hemispheres on a globe. Use the lamp to represent the sun as you explain and demonstrate the following information.

Explain that, in July, the sun's rays shine directly on the northern hemisphere. At the same time, the sun's rays shine at a slant on the southern hemisphere. Ask "Which hemisphere would be warmer?" Demonstrate this.

In December, the northern hemisphere is tilted away from the sun. The sun's rays hit it at a slant. At the same time, the sun's rays hit the southern hemisphere directly. Ask "Now which hemisphere would be warmer?" Demonstrate this.

Have your students look at the equator, or middle line, on the earth. Move the globe around the sun (*light bulb*) one more time. Ask "How does the light shine on the Equator?"

Changing Seasons

A Little Book

Reproduce the little book on page 7 for your students. (Before reproducing the page, put a mark on the globe on page 3 of the minibook to show where your class lives.) Have your students color the pictures, cut the four pages apart, and staple them to form a minibook.

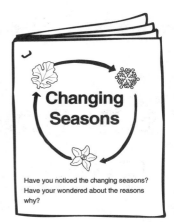

A Season Spinner

Materials:

- copy of page 8 for each student
- crayons
- watercolor wash and brush
- scissors
- glue
- hole punch
- 4 pieces of string - 12" long (30.5 cm)

Steps to follow:

1. Have students color the illustrations on the spinner with crayons, then cover the spinner with a watercolor wash. Let the spinner dry before doing step 2.

2. Cut out the spinner and fold on the dotted lines.

3. Fold down the top of the spinner along the "fold" line. Glue the flap to form a rectangle.

4. Punch holes where the pattern indicates. Attach one piece of string to each hole. Tie the four strings together at the other end. Spin.

Seasons Where You Live

Duplicate page 9 for your students. Help them to fill in the sections of the circle to identify the months when summer, winter, spring, and autumn occur in your community.

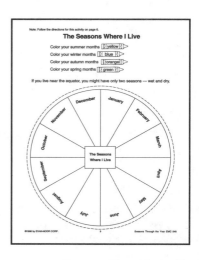

Changing Seasons

Have you noticed the changing seasons?
Have you wondered about the reasons
why?

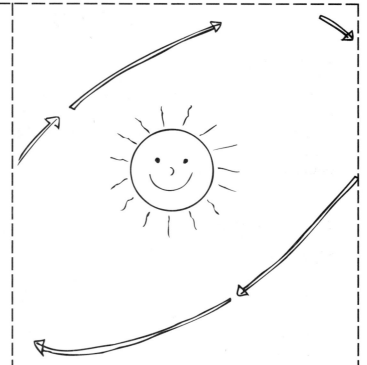

The earth moves around the sun in a
big circle called an **orbit**.

The sun shines on you.

Draw a line from the sun to the dot on
the earth that shows where you live.

The way the sun shines on the earth
changes as the earth moves around
the sun.

The same changes happen each year.
We call these changes **seasons**.

 fall

 winter

 spring

 summer

Note: Follow the directions on page 6 to have your students make a "season spinner." This spinner shows how seasons repeat in a pattern.

1. Color.   2. Paint.   3. Cut.   4. Fold.   5. Add strings.   6. Spin.

fold down for reinforcement

Autumn   **Winter**   **Spring**   **Summer**

glue

fold   fold   fold   fold

8   Seasons Through the Year EMC 548

The Seasons Where I Live

Color your summer months ⬛ yellow ⬛ ▷

Color your winter months ⬛ blue ⬛ ▷

Color your autumn months ⬛ orange ⬛ ▷

Color your spring months ⬛ green ⬛ ▷

If you live near the equator, you might have only two seasons — wet and dry.

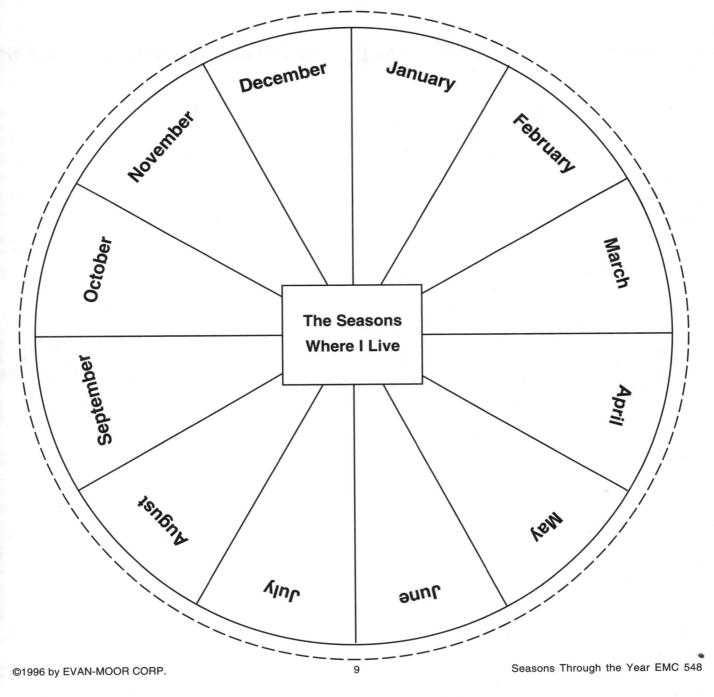

Note: Children love to hear a favorite story again and again. Read the story below several times practicing a different skill each time you read it.

The Mare on the Hill
by Thomas Locke
Dial Books, 1985

Day 1: Read *The Mare on the Hill*.

Discuss the story focusing on the action.

Day 2: Read *The Mare on the Hill*.

Focus on the time that passed during the story. Look for signs of seasons.

Day 3: Read *The Mare on the Hill*.

Write the events of the story on sentence strips. Help students read the strips. Have them arrange the events in order. Then have students match the events with the seasons in which they occurred. Encourage students to predict what will happen during the next year.

Some important story events:

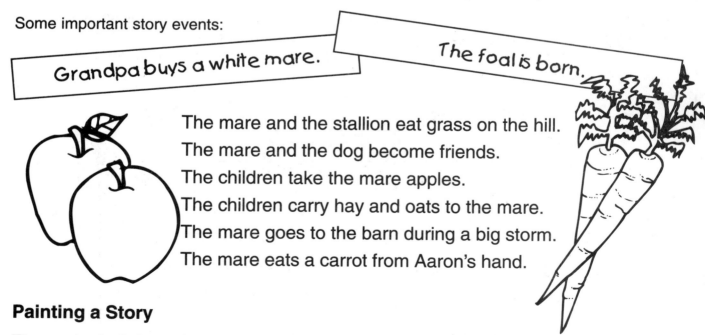

Grandpa buys a white mare.

The foal is born.

The mare and the stallion eat grass on the hill.
The mare and the dog become friends.
The children take the mare apples.
The children carry hay and oats to the mare.
The mare goes to the barn during a big storm.
The mare eats a carrot from Aaron's hand.

Painting a Story

Thomas Locker's beautiful paintings bring the seasons to life. Have your students paint a picture of something that happened to them. They should show the season by adding details to the background. Have students write or tell a story to go with their pictures.

 Seasons Through the Year EMC 548

Poetry for All Seasons

As you and your class explore the changing seasons, write free verse poems to record specific signs of the seasons. Use the word banks you will develop as you study the individual seasons. Students should dictate their ideas as you combine them into a class poem. Begin with the words "(Season name) is..." Encourage the class to use words that make "pictures" in the reader's mind.

Here is a sample verse about winter. It was written by first graders in Colorado.

Winter is mittens, coats, hats, scarves, boots, and snow pants,
Wearing warm clothes that make us feel like marshmallow men.

Winter is sinking into a soft, white bank and leaving footprints everywhere we go.
It's a slick, slippery sidewalk under our boots.

Winter is cold, white snow crystals falling on our heads
And the delicious wet spots they make on our tongues.

Winter is frosty flakes and slushy mush and dripping icicles.
Winter is a quiet, peaceful blanket covering the land.

Copy your students' class poems on colored paper. Surround the poems with illustrations made by the students. Hang the poems together for a permanent record of the "Changing Seasons." Read the panels often. Use the poetry for choral reading. Include student verses in your letters home to parents.

Seasonal Paper Dolls

Preparing Paper Dolls

Color and cut out the paper doll patterns found on pages 45 through 48. Laminate a set to be used as you discuss clothing worn for each season. Keep the pieces in a sturdy envelope between uses. Reproduce individual sets for students who want their own. You will need to provide help cutting out the clothing for younger students.

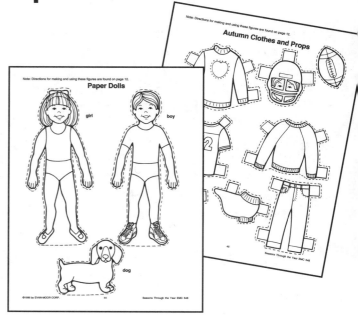

What Should I Wear When It Is _____?

As you study each season, display the dolls and a selection of their clothes. Ask your students to choose clothes that are appropriate for the particular season. Develop role- playing situations using the paper dolls. For example:

> *Sammy looks outside. What clothes will Sammy wear? What will he do?*
> *Susie has to pack a suitcase for an autumn trip. What should she pack?*

Autumn Days

Create an autumn scene on a sheet of butcher paper to use as a backdrop for the paper dolls. (Draw it yourself or have a group of children paint an autumn tree, clouds in the sky, etc.) Use the paper dolls and their props to finish the scene. Have children explain what the dolls are "doing." Repeat this activity for each season.

Story Time

Place a set of paper dolls along with their clothing and props in a "storytelling" center. Let pairs of students go to the center to tell each other stories using the paper dolls as characters. You may want to record some of these stories for other children to listen to at a later time.

What Is Autumn?

Creating a Word Bank

Brainstorm with your class to create a list of all the things that they think of when they hear the word *autumn* or the word *fall*. List the words and phrases on a giant chart. Keep the chart up during the balance of the unit as a word bank. Include activities that are specific to autumn where you live.

- *What do animals do?*
- *What do people do?*
- *What do trees do?*
- *What do farmers do?*

Autumn Words

autumn   squirrels

fall   colorful

leaves   cool days

wind   harvest

sweater   pumpkin

nuts   wind

September 10

Watching Changes Happen

Choose a tree near your school. Spend a few moments looking at the tree and talking about it. Have students draw the tree. Be sure to date the drawing. Look at the tree every week. Notice how the tree changes. Have the students draw the tree after each observation. Have students write or dictate a description of the changes. Have students keep their drawings and written pages in their unit journals or portfolios.

Autumn Where I Live

Duplicate the "Autumn Where I Live" form on page 14 for each student. Have them make a border that shows some of the signs of autumn that you have discussed. Then have students write or draw about their favorite part of autumn.

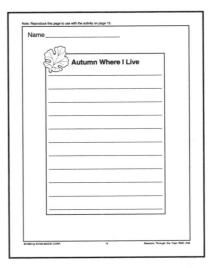

Note: Reproduce this page to use with the activity on page 13.

Name ____________________________

Autumn Where I Live

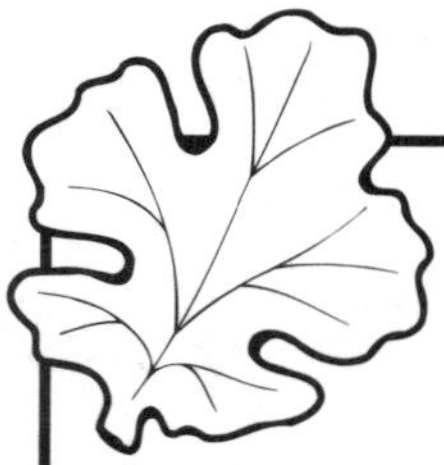

Autumn Math

One-to-One Correspondence

Put autumn objects in a basket. Show students number cards or math fact cards. Have them count out the appropriate number of items.

Addition and Subtraction Stories

Use the autumn objects to demonstrate story problems. Begin by telling some problems yourself and having students use the specimens to work out the answers. Have students write or tell the number sentence demonstrated as well as giving the correct answer. When your students are comfortable with the process, have them create their own problems. For example:

One day Sammy Squirrel was picking up nuts. He found three acorns and took them to his hole. Then he found two more acorns. How many acorns did Sammy find in all?

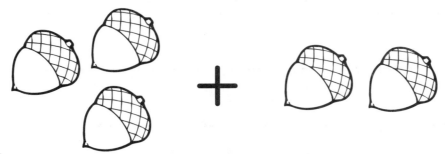

One More

Give each student a handful of autumn objects. Write a number on the chalkboard or show a number on a card. Have students show you that number plus one more. Vary the game by asking students to show one less, two more, etc.

3 and one more

Note: Vary the difficulty of these activities to fit the needs of your students.

Autumn Sorting and Patterning

Take your class on a nature walk to collect small autumn items such as leaves, grasses, seed pods, acorns, etc. Use this collection for the following activities:

Sorting Autumn

Have students sort the specimens into groups. Ask them to explain what attributes they used to create their groupings. For example:

The rule for these groups is leaves in a pile, sticks in a pile, and rocks in a pile.

The rule for these groups is big things in one group, small things in the other.

Autumn Patterning

Have students use the autumn objects to make patterns. After the pattern is made, ask the students to read the pattern and name it. The pattern can be glued to a strip of poster board.

Pointed leaf, round leaf , stick, pointed leaf, round leaf, stick.

This is an ABC pattern.

Autumn Patterns

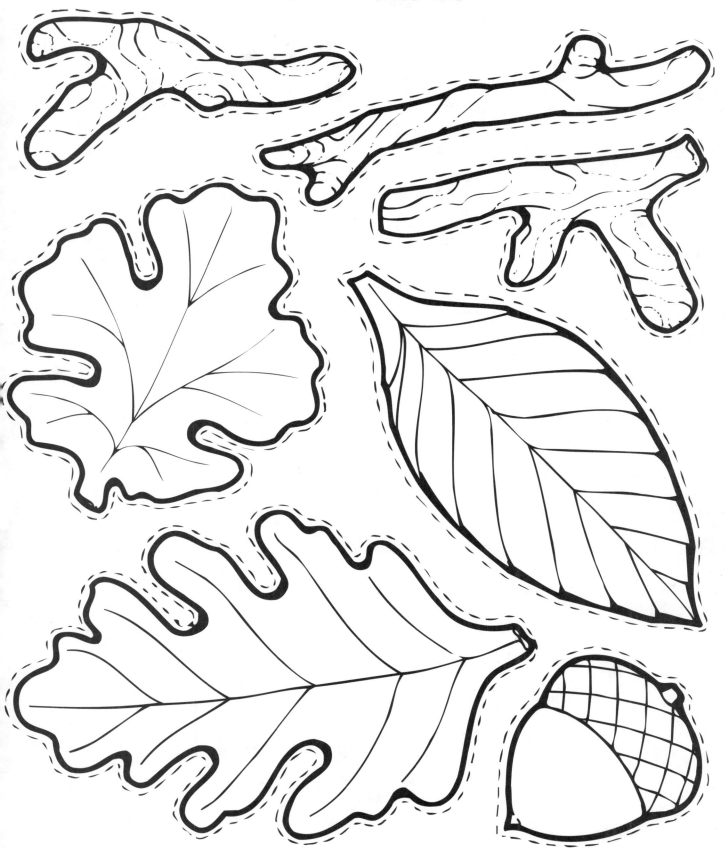

Note: Challenge your students to tell and write about leaves. Encourage them to write in several different genres. For example, children might write an observation, **Leaves in the Fall**, a story, **If I Were the Last Leaf on the Tree**, or a poem. Cut out the finished "leaves" and display.

Once Upon a Leaf

Tasting Autumn

Making Comparisons

In her poem "A Bowl of October" (**The Reading of Poetry**, Allyn & Bacon, 1966), Helen Bevington compares the fallen leaves to Cornflakes® and Wheaties®. Discuss with your class how dried leaves are like breakfast cereals. Bring in a variety of cereals for children to see. Have your students make comparisons. (Shredded wheat looks like bales of hay. Puffed cereal looks like the end of a cattail.) Record the comparisons on a class chart.

A Taste Test

Set up a taste test with the different cereals. Display the boxes of cereal. Have each student taste a flake or nugget of each cereal. Students should choose their favorite. Make this symbolic graph to show class preferences. Provide an empty paper bowl for each cereal tasted. Give each student a plastic spoon. When students have chosen their favorite, they put their spoon into the bowl representing that cereal. As soon as students have finished, discuss the graph by asking questions such as:

- Which cereal was the most popular?
- How many people liked it?
- Which cereal was the least popular?
- How many more people liked the most popular cereal than the least popular one?

Questions should reflect the readiness level of your class. Save the results of your test by gluing the bowls and spoons to a sheet of poster board.

A Bulletin Board

A class "bowl of autumn" makes a great bulletin board. Have students imagine that all of the activities they enjoy during the fall are in a giant bowl. Brainstorm with your class to create a list of their favorites. List them on the board or on a chart.

Have students draw and cut out pictures of themselves participating in favorite fall activities. Put a large paper bowl on a bulletin board and fill it with these cutouts. Accent the bowl with real or paper leaves.

A Bowl of Autumn

 Seasons Through the Year EMC 548

More Autumn Fun

An Autumn Frame-Up

To preserve the beautiful autumn days, take a photo of your class outdoors. You might want them to pose in front of the tree that you watched as it changed. Make a posterboard frame for the picture. Select a group of children to glue leaves, seed pods, etc., to the frame. Post the picture in your room. Take another picture in the same spot during each of the other seasons. Post the pictures together and invite comparisons.

Way Down Yonder

Cut out paper leaves or use real leaves for this action song. Fill a basket with the leaves. Walk around the room dropping the leaves from the basket as you sing this version of "Way Down Yonder in the Paw-Paw Patch." Fill in the blanks with students' names.

> *Where, oh where, is dear little _____?*
> *Where, oh where, is dear little _____?*
> *Where, oh where, is dear little _____?*
> *Way down yonder by the big oak tree.*

When the verse is finished, the students chosen begin picking up the leaves that you've dropped as you sing.

> *There's little _____ picking up leaves.*
> *There's little _____ picking up leaves.*
> *There's little _____ picking up leaves.*
> *Way down yonder by the big oak tree.*

Repeat to include all students.

What Is Winter?

A Winter Word Bank

Brainstorm with your class to create a list of all the things that are a part of winter. Write the words on a large chart. Have students categorize the ideas on the list according to their senses. Putting the words in categories helps to stimulate more words.

Things I See	Things I Hear	Things I Smell	Things I Taste	Things I Feel
snowflakes sleds	wind blowing puppy barking	pine trees wet socks	soup hot chocolate	furry mittens cold ice

Make a Coatrack Graph

During the winter, most people wear warm clothes such as coats, hats, and gloves. Make this "coatrack" graph following these directions. First sort all the different types of items found on your coatrack or in your closet (coats, hats, mittens, boots, scarves, sweaters, backpacks, etc.).

Make a **real graph** by laying the items out on the floor as if in a grid. Then make a **symbolic graph**. List the categories on the board. Have students write their name on a small strip of paper. Students will put their name by each type of item that they have. If they have items in more than one category, they should put up two names.

Spend some time discussing the graph when it is complete. Ask the class to tell you something they know after looking at the graph. Accept any reasonable answer. Then question the group to illicit any conclusions that they might have overlooked.

Winter Where I Live

Duplicate the "Winter Where I Live" form on page 22. Have students make a border that shows some signs of winter, and then write or draw to show their favorite part of winter.

Note: Reproduce this page to use with the activity on page 21.

Name ______________________________

Winter Where I Live

Mitten Math

Copycats

Show a pair of patterned mittens to your class. Point out that each mitten has the same pattern. The mittens are "copycats." Pin up two large construction paper mittens to demonstrate mitten symmetry. Paste a colored shape on one mitten. Have a student paste the same shape in the same spot on the other mitten. Continue until the large mittens are well decorated.

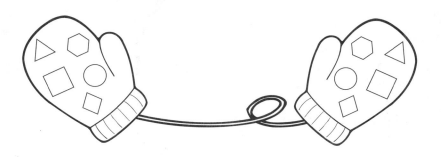

Provide students with two hand-sized paper mittens (see page 24). Have them glue or d raw shapes to decorate one of their mittens. Then have them make the other mitten a "copycat" of the first mitten. Tape a piece of yarn between each pair of mittens and display them around the big mittens you did as a class.

A Mitten Pattern

Give students copies of the mitten strips on page 24. Have them color the mittens in the strip to create a pattern. For example:

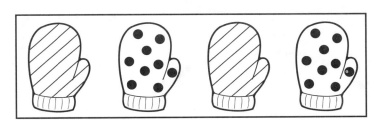

If your students have had a lot of experience patterning, have them glue two strips together for more complex patterns. Then challenge them to color and position the mittens so that their new strips show at least two pattern elements.

"Show Me" with Mittens

Cut out the small mittens to use as individual counters. Give each student a set of the mittens. Use the mittens as you would other math counters. Ask a question and have students show you the answer with their mitten counters.

Show me 3 + 2.

Show me 9.

Show me one more than 7.

Show me 5 - 0.

$$3 + 2$$

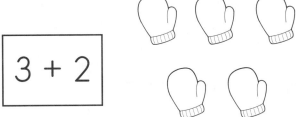

Note: Reproduce these patterns to use with math activities on page 23.

Mitten Patterns

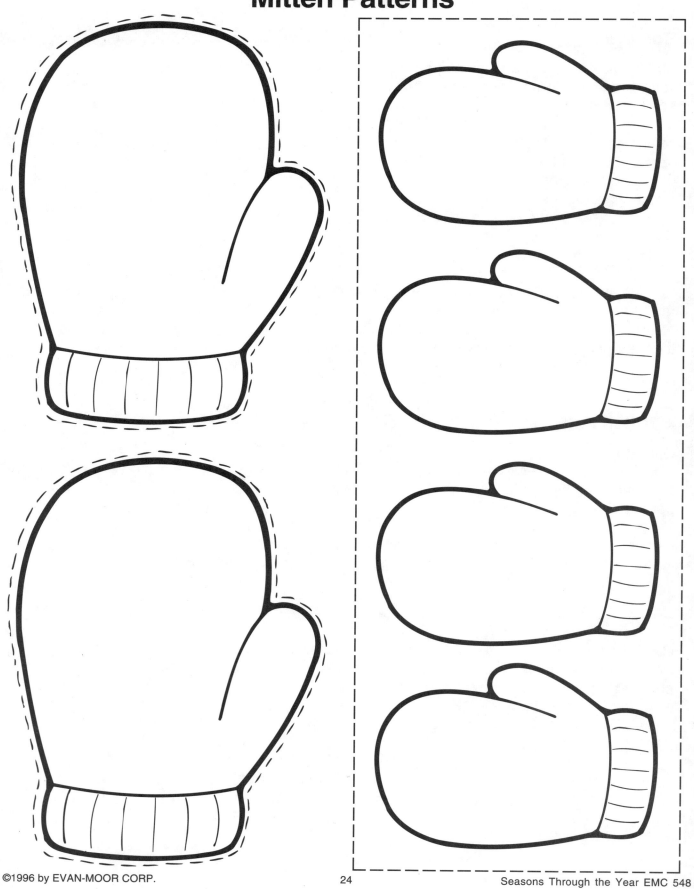

24

Seasons Through the Year

The tree beside my kitchen doc
has buds on it and a robin's nes
I think of all the seasons,
spring must be the very best.

The tree beside my kitchen doc

Autumn

has green leaves shining in the s

Robin babies flap and call,

"Come out and play. It's summe

The tree beside my kitchen doo

dropped all it's leaves upon the

The robin's have flown to a warr

now that autumn is around.

The tree beside my kitchen doo

becomes a white and solemn g

As frost and snow in the frozen

blanket my winter yard.

Dress for

Mittens in Literature

Day 1:

Read **The Mitten** as retold by Alvin Tresselt (Lothrop, Lee & Shepard, 1966).

Ask your students to recall what the mitten looked like. Have them help you create a list of the animals that lived in the mitten. Discuss what happened to the mitten.

Day 2:

Read **The Mitten, an Old Ukrainian Folk Tale**, as retold by Jan Brett (Putnam, 1989.)

Note the mitten's description, the animals that lived in the mitten, and what happened to the mitten. Compare the ways in which Jan Brett's version and Alvin Tresselt's version are similar and how they are different.

Day 3:

Write your own classroom version of the mitten following this story pattern.

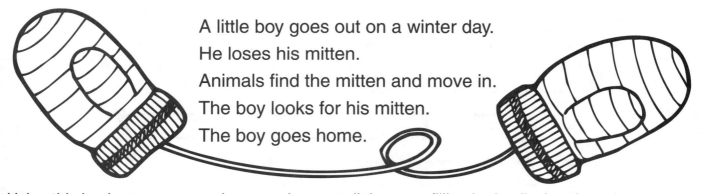

A little boy goes out on a winter day.
He loses his mitten.
Animals find the mitten and move in.
The boy looks for his mitten.
The boy goes home.

Using this basic story pattern, have students retell the story filling in details that they choose. Copy the story onto large sheets of paper and have individual students illustrate each page. If possible, make small copies of your class version for each student to illustrate and read.

After the class has completed their version, compare it with the two versions you read to the class.

Lost Mittens

What would happen if you
lost your mitten?
Write or tell about it.

Snow

Snow Hunt

Take a walk just after a snowstorm to see where the snow has landed. When you return to the classroom, record where you saw the snow. You might sketch a basic map of your school and draw in where you found snow, or just record words that describe the snowy places.

Take the same walk several days later to see what changes have occurred in the snow. When you return to the classroom, record where you saw the changes in the snow. Compare the two snow hunts. What differences did you see? What caused the differences?

Saving a Snow Ball

In Ezra Jack Keat's *A Snowy Day* (Scholastic Inc., 1962), the little boy tries unsuccessfully to keep a snowball in his pocket. Discuss where snowballs could be saved successfully in your classroom. Make snowballs and try out the places that are suggested. (If you don't have snow in your area, you can used shaved ice to make snowballs for this experiment.) The snowballs should all be the same size and should be placed in bowls. Have students check the snowballs often and keep a log to show what happens. Ask students to describe what kind of place is good for preventing snowball meltdown.

Have students complete the form "Where to Keep a Snowball" found at the bottom of this page. Challenge them to think of a place at home, other than the freezer, where a snowball could be kept. Encourage them to test their ideas at home and report the results to the class.

Where to Keep a Snowball

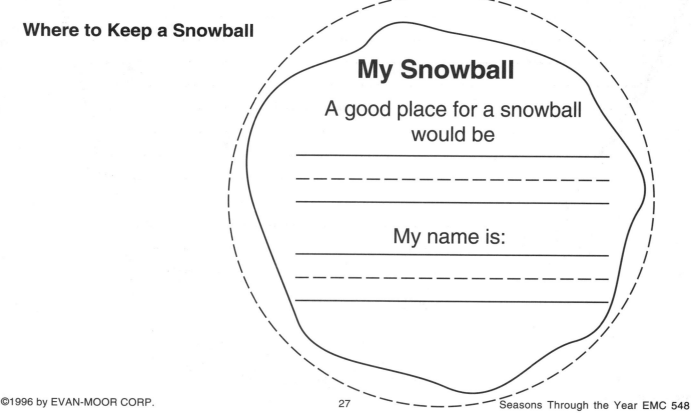

My Snowball

A good place for a snowball would be

_____

_____

My name is:

_____

Note: If you live in an area where water will not freeze when placed outside during the winter, make these frozen pictures in the freezer.

Ice Pictures

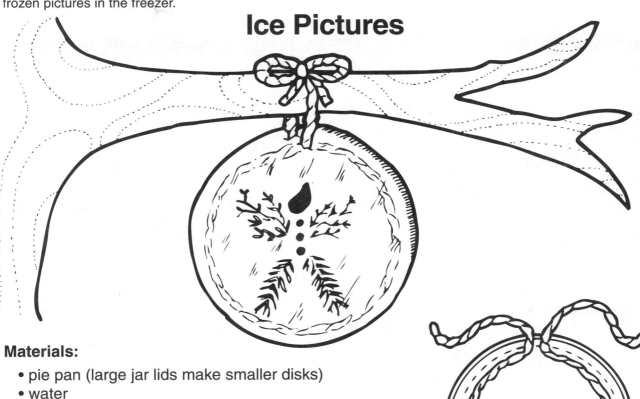

Materials:

- pie pan (large jar lids make smaller disks)
- water
- yarn
- sprigs of evergreen, berries, nuts, small pebbles, beans, etc.

What to Do:

1. Fill a pie pan with water and line the edge of the pan with yarn. Leave enough yarn out of the water at the top to tie around a branch or hook.

2. Put sprigs of evergreen and berries into the water. Arrange them so that they make a picture.

3. Put the pan on a flat surface outside until the water freezes and the yarn and decorations are locked in the ice.

4. Remove the pan. (If you have trouble, dip the pan in warm water as you would to remove gelatin from a mold.)

5. Hang the disk from a branch outside and watch the sun sparkle through your ice picture.

Different shaped ice pictures can be made by varying the shape of the container.

 Seasons Through the Year EMC 548

What Is Spring?

A Spring Word Bank

Brainstorm to create a class list of spring words. Make the word bank in the form of a giant bouquet with a word on each flower. If you have categorized your words, all one category could go on the same color flower.

Mud

As snow melts, ground thaws, and rains fall, MUD becomes a sign of spring. Set up a "mud center" in your classroom. Minimize the mess by putting a plastic tablecloth on the floor under the working area and covering the table with another plastic cloth. Provide measuring cups, bowls, spoons, water, and dirt. A tub of warm soapy water or a sink and lots of paper towels are a necessity.

Before students begin working at the center, set up guidelines for appropriate behavior. For example:

> *Water and dirt must remain in bowls.*
> *Work on your own mud.*
> *Clean up the center area before returning to your class work.*

Challenge students to write a recipe for good mud. They should measure the dirt and the water and stir to mix well. Have them record the measurements for their mud recipes on the card form on page 30. Recipes will vary. Some people like their mud "gooshy" and some like it firm.

If you are rotating groups through the center, provide an empty trash can marked *Mud Dump*. Have students dump mud into the can before cleaning up.

Muddy Verses

Have students list words that describe mud. Then have each student choose four descriptive words from the list to write on the form on page 30 to make his/her mud verse.

Spring Where You Live

Duplicate the "Spring Where I Live" form on page 31. Have students make a border that shows some of the signs of spring, and then write or draw to show their favorite part of spring.

Note: Use this form to write a recipe for mud following the directions on page 29.

mud

My Recipe for Mud

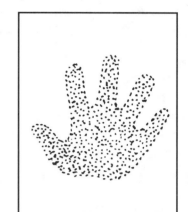

_____ 's of dirt

_____ 's of water

Mix well!

Note: Use this card to write a "Mud Verse" following the directions on page 29.

_____,

_____,

_____,

_____,

mud!

Name _____

Spring Where I Live

Seed Center Math

Spring is a time for planting and growing. Use seeds as the focus of several math lessons and then plant them to watch them grow.

Set up a seed center. Buy several packages of seeds. Glue several seeds from each package onto a small paper plate (one plate for each kind of seed). Write the name of the seeds on the back of the plate. Dump the remaining seeds from the package into a large shallow bowl. Keep the seed packet for planting instructions and matching games. Students can complete the following jobs at the "Seed Center."

Sorting Seeds

Have students take a handful of seeds from the large bowl and sort them. Provide paper medicine cups or small paper plates to hold the sorted seeds. Have students make a record of their handful by tracing around their own hand and drawing a circle on the traced hand for each kind of seed. They should glue one of the seeds in each circle to label it. Then students should record the number of seeds that they had in each circle.

Biggest to Smallest

Have students arrange the seeds in order from biggest seed to smallest seed. Ask them "Will the big seed grow into a big plant?" Discuss their ideas. When you plant the seeds, be sure to address this question.

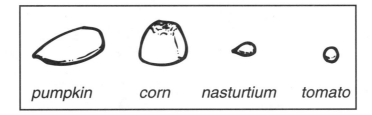

pumpkin   corn   nasturtium   tomato

Seed Counters

Practice math computation using seeds as counters. Try addition with three or more addends by "planting" a row of seeds. Say, "If I plant two seeds in one hole, three seeds in another hole, and one seed in my last hole, how many seeds did I plant in the row?

Spring Gardens

Seed Packets

Share the directions on a seed packet with your class. Explain the purpose of each section. Read several packets and compare the information. Share information appropriate for your class. For example, "This plant grows in 15 days" or "You have to plant this seed 1 inch (2.5 cm) deep."

Plant Your Gardens

Plant seeds and watch them grow. Record in a "plant journal" the number of days it takes for each seed to germinate. Have students observe to answer the question, "Do different seeds of the same type take different amounts of time?"

Here are some planting tips:

Cut the tops off half-pint milk cartons and wash them well to provide containers for the soil. Poke several holes in the bottom of each carton and cover it with a layer of gravel. Fill the cartons with potting soil, moisten the soil with water, and press it down firmly. Plant tiny seeds like radishes, grass, and parsley by placing them on the surface and then scratching the surface to cover them just slightly. Plant seeds like peas and beans about an inch deep. Keep the soil moist all the time.

Some seeds may sprout in a few days and other seeds may take weeks to sprout. The sprouts will have two round or oval leaves at the top, which look nothing like the plant's typical leaves. From between these, the first true leaves will grow.

When a seedling has grown several pair of true leaves, it is old enough to be transplanted. Prepare clay or plastic pots for transplanting. A container four inches across the top and at least that high is a good starting size.

When the plants grow too big for these pots, you can always move them to larger containers or transplant them outside. Fill the containers with soil, moisten the soil, and press it down somewhat. Make a finger deep hole in the soil in the middle of the pot. Gently, pick up each seedling and put it into the prepared hole. Push the surrounding soil snugly against the seedlings.

Note: Reproduce the flowers on this page for patterning and sorting. The patterns can also be used to create a "spring" garden. Have children make a "cat-spring," then glue a flower pattern at one end and paste the other end to a square of construction paper. When students push down on the top of the flower it will "spring" back.

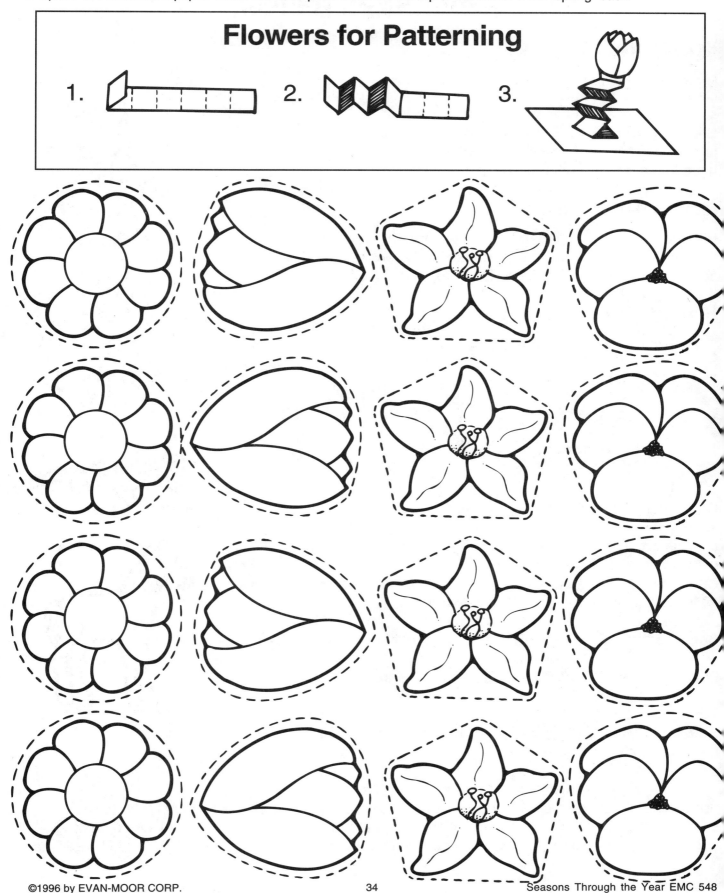

Flowers for Patterning

1.　　　　　2.　　　　　3.

　　　　34

Note: Read **Ruth Heller's Chickens Aren't the Only Ones** (Grosset & Dunlap, 1981) and **Babies Born Alive and Well** (Grosset & Dunlap, 1982). As a bonus activity, have students put an x on the animals on this page that are **oviparous**.

Parents and Babies

Spring is a time of new baby animals.

Match the babies with their parents.

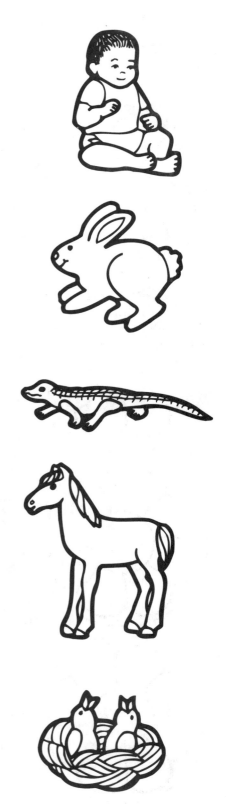

35   Seasons Through the Year EMC 548

What is Summer?

Summer Word Bank

Brainstorm to create a list of words about summer. Words for summer might be grouped as "indoor words and outdoor words" or "working words and playing words."

Summer Fun

Stamp and clap to this simple chant. March to the words.

> *Play and run*
> *In the summer sun.*
> *Skip and turn.*
> *It's summer fun.*

Have students add phrases to tell things they do during the summer. Write these chants on the chalkboard.

Splash in the pool
In the summer sun.
Drink lemonade.
It's summer fun.

After the group oral work, have students tell or write their own "Summer Fun" verses. Have them illustrate their verses. Bind the verses together to create a class book.

Butterfly Net

In this game, four students will be the "butterfly net." They hold hands in a line. All other students are "butterflies" and flit around waving their hands up and down. The "net" chases the "butterflies" and tries to catch one by surrounding it. Butterflies that are caught become part of the net. The "net' continues to try to catch the other "butterflies." The last four butterflies become a new net.

Summer Where I Live

Duplicate the "Summer Where I Live" form on page 37. Have students make a border that shows some of the summer activities that you have discussed, then write or draw to show their favorite part of summer.

Note: Reproduce this page to use with the activity on page 36.

Name ______________________________

Summer Where I Live

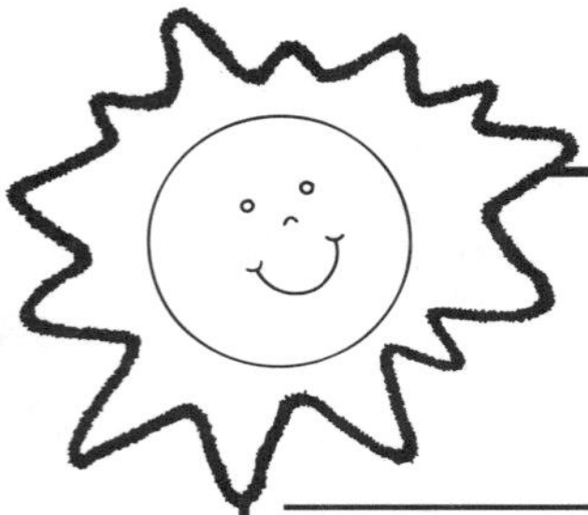

Melon Math

Choose a medium-sized watermelon to use for the following activities.

How Much Does It Weigh?

Have students watch as you weigh a small object such as a potato or a book. Then weigh a heavy object such as a child or a box of blocks. Students should each lift the small object and watermelon. Ask "Which weighs more? Does the watermelon weigh more or less than the heavy object?"

Ask students to estimate how much the watermelon weighs. Record their estimates, then weigh the watermelon.

How Big Around is it?

Have students watch as you measure the circumference of a playground ball with a string or long strip of paper. Tell them that you are making a "belt" for the ball that goes around the middle. Show the length of the "belt."

Now have students estimate the length of string needed for the watermelon's "belt." When everyone has had a chance to estimate, let students try the belts on the watermelon. Tape the strings to a poster arranging them in groups titled "Too Long," "Too Short," and "Just Right."

How Many Seeds?

Have students estimate the number of seeds that will be in the watermelon. Then cut the watermelon and serve each student a piece. Provide a plate or napkin for the watermelon and a plate for collecting seeds. Students should save their seeds as they eat the watermelon.

When they are finished eating, have students count the seeds on their seed plates and them arrange the plates in a real graph to show how many seeds were on each plate. Spend some time discussing the graph. Then add up the total number of seeds to determine how many seeds the whole watermelon had.

Watermelon Patterning and Sorting

Reproduce the watermelon patterns on page 39 to use for patterning and sorting activities.

Note: Reproduce these patterns to use with the activity on page 38.

Watermelon Patterns

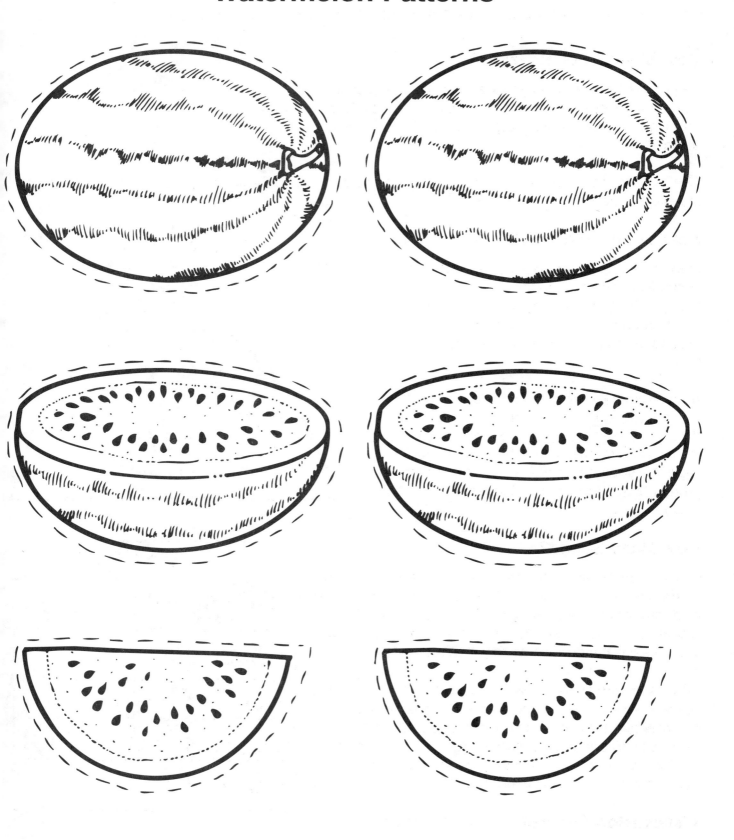

39

The Shining Sun
A Watercolor Resist

Your room will seem to radiate sunshine as you post these colorful suns.

Materials:

- squares of white paper
- crayons
- watercolor paints - orange, yellow, and red
- brushes
- water

Follow these steps:

1. Draw a circle on the white paper with a crayon. Press firmly.

2. Decorate the outer edge of the circle with a pattern of rays. Give the sun a smiling face.

3. Fill in some areas using crayon. Leave some areas uncolored.

4. Paint over the sun with a watercolor wash. Continue until the whole sun is covered. Make all the brushstrokes in the same direction. Once an area is painted, do not go back and repaint it. Let the painting dry.

5. Cut out the sun, leaving a narrow border around the drawing.

6. Mount the sun on black construction paper. Trim the paper so that a border of black surrounds the painting. Hang from the ceiling or display on a bulletin board.

Fun in the Sun

A Sunny Finger Play

See that sun,
That big ol' sun.
It shines right down on me.

See that sun,
That big ol' sun.
It's happy as can be.

See that sun,
That big ol' sun
It helps to make things grow.

See that sun,
That big ol' sun.
I'm sad to see it go.

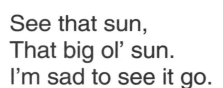

Rabbits in the Sun

All players pretend to be rabbits and hop about. The leader calls "Danger" and all the rabbits freeze perfectly still until they hear the call "Danger past." Any rabbit that wobbles or wiggles during the time of danger is out of the game and must go to the a resting area (the "hutch") for the next turn.

The Colors of the Year

Autumn is orange and yellow and brown.
Watch as all the leaves fall down.

- -

Winter is white with cheeks of red.
I watch it while I snuggle in bed.

Spring is green and pink and blue.
It's filled with growing things so new.

Summer paints a rainbow across the sky
And in my garden, paints a butterfly.

Note: Directions for making and using these figures are found on page 12.

Paper Dolls

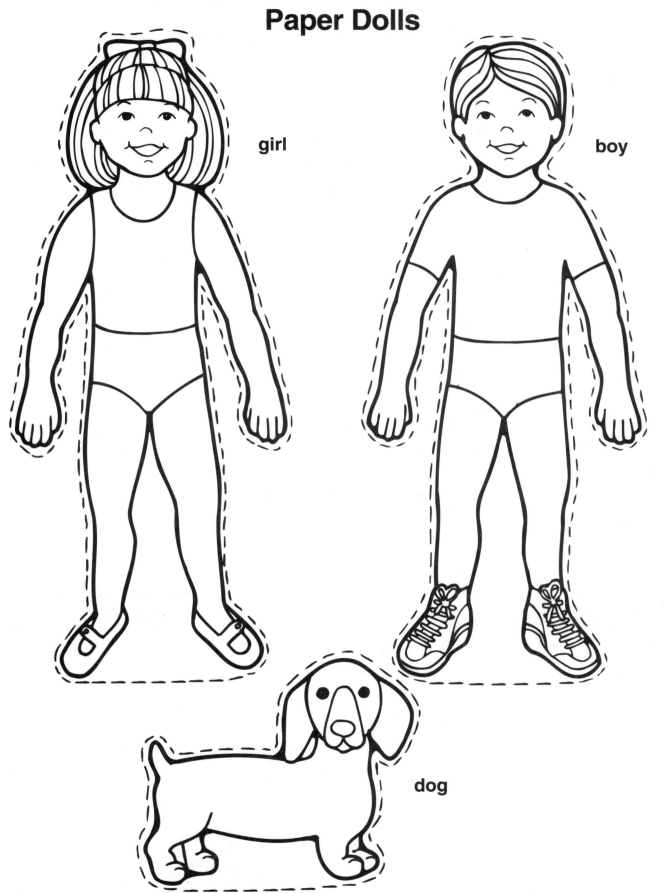

girl

boy

dog

44

Note: Directions for making and using these figures are found on page 12.

Autumn Clothes and Props

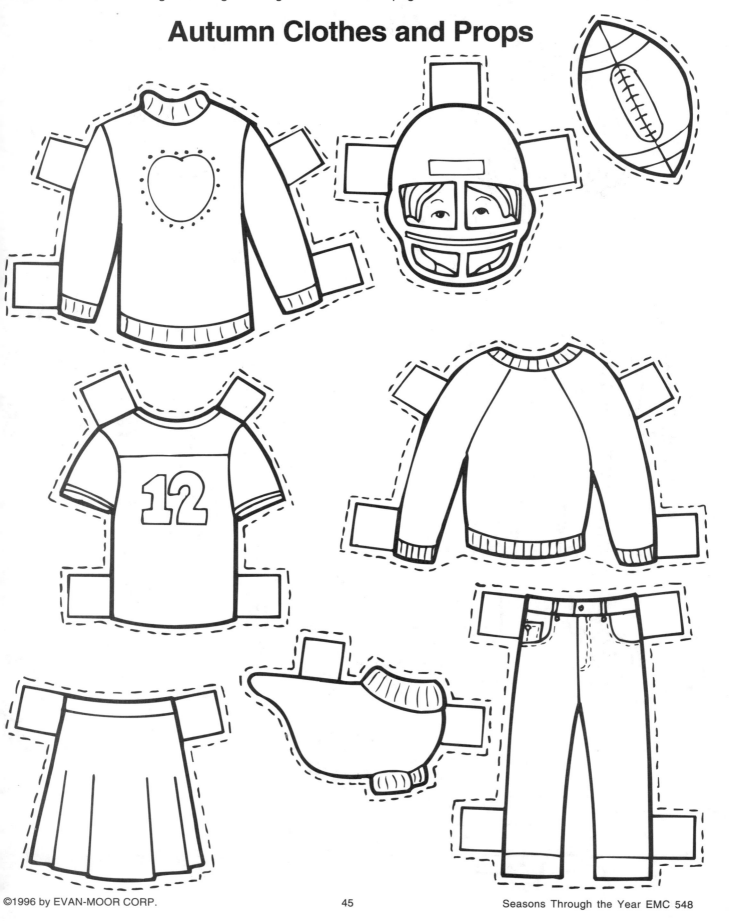

Winter Clothes and Props

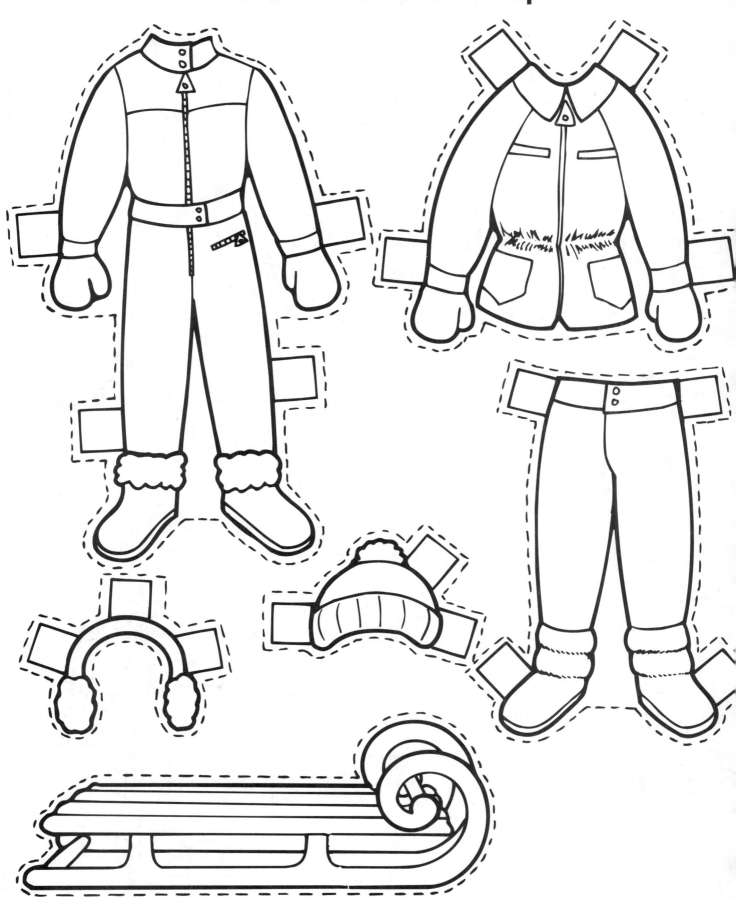

Spring Clothes and Props

Note: Directions for making and using these figures are found on page 12.

Summer Clothes and Props

Bone

48

Jill Norris

Autumn

Winter

Winter

Summer

Spring

Summer